The Everything Book of DOGS & PUPPIES

Penguin
Random
House

Senior Editor **Carrie Love**
Senior Designer **Karen Hood**
US Editor **Jane Perlmutter**
US Senior Editor **Shannon Beatty**
Editors **Jolyon Goddard and Katy Lennon**
Author **Andrea Mills**
Consultant **Bruce Fogle MBE DVM MRCVS**
Pre-Production Producer **Dragana Puvacic**
Senior Producer **Amy Knight**
Jacket Designer **Eleanor Bates**
Jacket Coordinator **Francesca Young**
Creative Technical Support **Sonia Charbonnier**
Managing Editors **Deborah Lock
and Penny Smith**
Managing Art Editor **Mabel Chan**
Publisher **Mary Ling**
Art Director **Jane Bull**

First American Edition, 2018
Published in the United States by DK Publishing
1450 Broadway, Suite 801, New York, NY 10018

Copyright © 2018 Dorling Kindersley Limited
DK, a Division of Penguin Random House LLC
20 21 10 9 8 7 6 5 4 3
004–308554–Jun/2018

A catalog record for this book
is available from the Library of Congress.
ISBN 978-1-4654-7010-2

DK books are available at special discounts when
purchased in bulk for sales promotions, premiums,
fund-raising, oreducational use. For details, contact: DK
Publishing Special Markets, 1450 Broadway, Suite 801,
New York, NY 10018 SpecialSales@dk.com

Printed in China

A WORLD OF IDEAS:
SEE ALL THERE IS TO KNOW
www.dk.com

Contents

Welcome to
the wonderful
world of dogs
and puppies!

World of dogs

Dogs are part of the canine family. They are found on six of the world's continents. Some live in the **wild**, while others are **pets**.

Chihuahua   Alaskan Malamute

North America is home to a range of domestic dogs. The Chihuahua is from Mexico. It's the world's smallest dog.

Wolves

The biggest members of the canine family are wolves. They have big teeth for chewing.

Gray Wolf

North America

Foxes

Foxes are natural hunters. They have bushy tails and their fur is usually red.

Some pet dogs look similar to wild wolves!

Maned Wolf

South America

Pet dogs

Domestic dogs are kept as pets. There are hundreds of different breeds.

Dachshund   **Norwegian Elkhound**

A range of different domestic dogs are kept as pets in Europe.

Chow Chow   **Tibetan Mastiff**   **Shih Tzu**

The dogs of Asia are varied. They have different characteristics depending on whether they live in deserts, forests, or mountains.

Red Fox

Europe

Asia

Silky Terrier   Australian Cattle Dog

Dingoes, wild dogs, and domestic breeds live here.

Dhole

African Hunting Dog

Africa

Dogs from Africa have short fur to keep cool.

Boerboel   **Basenji**

Peruvian Hairless   **Fila Brasileiro**

A variety of pet dogs, many stray dogs, and wild dogs all inhabit South America.

Dingo

Australia

There are **36 species** in the canine family.

Little and **large**

Some dogs can grow taller than their owners! An adult Great Dane can be more than 50 times heavier than an adult Chihuahua, the world's smallest dog breed.

Great Dane
These **gentle giants** are from **Germany**.

Big dogs

need lots of room at home and plenty of exercise. They like long walks.

Medium-sized

dogs don't take up as much room at home, but also need long walks.

Small dogs

take up the least room at home, but they also love long walks.

A fully grown male Great Dane is 28–30 in (71–76 cm) tall.

The **Great Dane** is the world's **biggest** dog.

Chihuahua

Bold and alert, this tiny breed grows to just 6–9 in (15–23 cm) tall and makes a great companion.

The tail is carried up or over the back.

Doggie design

Our **four-legged friends** belong to the **canine** family, made up of wolves, foxes, and wild dogs. Dogs are known for their **instincts** to herd, hunt, and guard.

Eyes Dogs have very big eyes and supersharp eyesight.

Tails Dogs have tails to help them balance when running.

Bones Most dogs are built for speed. This skeleton shows the flexible spine and long legs.

Legs Strong and muscular legs are good for running.

Ears
Dogs' ears move around to pick up sounds.

Tongues
Taste buds on the tongue detect if food is good to eat.

Paws
Dogs' paws have claws for gripping. Dogs also sweat through their paws.

Rolling
Dogs roll in smelly stuff as wild dogs once did. This covers their scent and tricks their prey.

Panting
Dogs only sweat through their paws, so panting keeps them cool. This is why their tongues are often out!

Playing
Dogs love toys and playtime because their brainpower is the same as a two-year-old child.

Family life

Welcome to the world! A mother's love sees her newborn puppies through their first weeks, with a lot of carrying, cleaning, and feeding.

Birth to 1 week old

Newborn puppies spend a whopping 90 percent of the time asleep! Their favorite thing is nursing mom's milk.

The mother dog supplies milk for the first eight weeks of a pup's life.

2–3 weeks old

As the eyes open for the first time, the fun starts! Puppies learn fast by copying mommy.

3–4 weeks old

Puppies now have a sense of smell. They play together and can go to the bathroom without help from mom.

✔ Top tip

When **picking a puppy** to bring home, look for more **confident pups** enjoying **playtime**. Shy puppies may be difficult to take care of.

The average litter ranges from three to nine puppies.

6 weeks old

Puppies stop nursing mom's milk and now eat solid food. This is called weaning.

11

Puppy
power!

The early stages of life are a big learning time, when pups find out about the world and others.

Top training
Making sure your puppy is well-trained from a young age will encourage good behavior.

Playing your part
The way a dog behaves in adulthood comes from its life as a puppy.

Playing by the rules
As puppies play together, they learn new rules and the best ways to behave.

Regular routines
Puppies need repeated routines with regular training, feeding, and playing to become confident dogs.

✔ **Top tip**

Taking time with **socialization** during the **first year** of life results in a **confident** pet dog.

Social start

It is important for puppies to spend time with different people and animals. This is called socialization. Begin with short walks and build up to longer walks in new places. Research shows that puppies with limited experience can have problems as adults, such as feeling scared or biting strangers.

Don't worry, pup. You'll be much taller soon!

Hmmm... is this my dinner?

Pooch parlor

Check out this good-looking bunch! There is never a **bad hair day** at the pooch parlor, where dog coats come in different colors, patterns, textures, and thicknesses.

Canine combs

Choose a medium-toothed comb for general grooming, a fine-toothed comb for thin hair, or a wide-toothed comb for thicker hair.

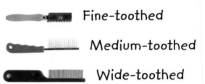

Fine-toothed

Medium-toothed

Wide-toothed

Hair care

Dalmatian

Yorkshire Terrier

Short coat

Long coat

This is the easiest coat to take care of. Daily brushing, and a good grooming once a week using a hair dryer on low heat, is all you need to remove dead hair. Give this dog a bath every three months.

Attention is needed with a long coat. Daily grooming prevents tangles. Remove big knots with a strong comb, and get rid of smaller tangles with a slicker brush.

Dog brushes
A slicker brush is the best all-around brush. Go for a curry brush on short hair or a pin brush on long hair.

Shampoo
Use special dog shampoo and conditioner to clean the fur.

Hair clippers
If your dog's coat needs to be clipped, ask a grown-up to use an electric clipper.

Nail clippers
Dog toenail clippers keep a dog's paws neat and tidy.

Curry brush

Pin brush

Slicker brush

Shampoo

Clippers

Toenail clippers

Wire Fox Terrier

Wiry coat

Poodle

Curly coat

Wiry and curly coats do not shed as much hair as other coats. Go to an experienced dog groomer twice a year for hand-stripping dead hair. Between visits, trim with scissors or clippers to keep your furry friend in top condition.

His **nose** knows!

Sniff! A dog's sense of smell is like its own **superpower**. It is 60 times stronger than a human's sense of smell, so a dog can smell lots of things that we can't.

A human fingerprint

A dog's nose is like its own built-in identity tag.

DOG TAG ID

Nose-print ID

Every dog has a different pattern of lines on its nose, just like every person has a different fingerprint.

Wet nose

Moist, drippy noses can help a dog pick up smells even better. A wet nose also keeps a dog cool.

✔ Top tip

On walks, let dogs take time to **sniff things**, so they **don't lose** their **superpower**.

A dog's nose has 300 million smell receptors, but a human nose has only 6 million.

Mmm! Dinner smells good. Hope it's for me!

Whiskers help a dog figure out the size and shape of nearby objects.

Invisible smells
Dogs use smell to find out if other animals are friendly.

Moving smells
Dogs know smells move around and become faint over time.

Strong smells
Dogs love to check out strong smells, like your smelly boots!

Ear emotions

Dogs have a **super sense** of **hearing**, but they can also **express** different feelings by the **position** of their ears.

Did I just hear "Walk!"? I'm coming!

Hear, hear!

Dogs can hear about four times better than we can, and detect much quieter sounds than us.

Ears prick up to follow the direction of sounds.

Did you know?

All puppies are born deaf because their ear canals are closed.

All ears

Dog ears are all different shapes and sizes. Muscles inside the ears mean dogs can tilt, turn, raise, and lower them. Some ears move much more than others. Here are the main types of ears:

Pricked—pointing upward

Semipricked

Bat—large and upright

Droopy and floppy

Rose—skin folded backward

Pooch panel

The ears have it! Guess how each pooch is feeling by the position of their ears...

Ears raised forward
Oh dear! This dog is feeling angry, and it is best to steer clear.

Ears held naturally
Happy days! This dog is feeling content, relaxed, and comfortable.

Ears pulled back
Please pay attention to me! This dog is showing it is friendly and approachable.

Ears raised high
What has caught this dog's attention? The ears suggest strong interest.

Ears flat down
Here is one worried woofer. Flat ears mean the dog feels scared.

19

"Tell-tail" signs

Dogs use their tails to express emotions. Whether short and stumpy or long and fluffy, the tail is the best indicator of how your doggie's day is going.

30

Speed **check:**

Superfast wag =
threatened dog

Fast wag =
friendly dog

Slow wag =
content dog

Small wag =
nervous dog

Chasing tails
Dogs are often seen chasing their own tails. This can be for fun or for exercise. Very fast chasing could mean fleas though, so check their fur!

Tail talk

Wagging tail
Here's a happy fella! This type of tail suggests the dog is feeling happy and excited, but also check that the face looks relaxed to be sure.

Tucked tail
When the tail is tucked under the body, the dog is feeling scared or worried. It is best to give this pooch some space.

A happy dog swings its tail to the right, but an unhappy dog swings it to the left!

Approach a new dog with a **grown-up**.

Upright tail
Something has caught this dog's eye. The tail stands upright to show excitement and interest. A chase could be on!

Straight tail
This tail is doing the talking! The dog is alert and defensive. A straight tail means the dog feels threatened.

Yaps and barks!

From whining woofers to breathless barkers, dogs like to make themselves heard! But listen closely to these sounds and you'll learn what they mean.

Standing up on two legs shows excitement and interest.

Doggie talk

Yap
A repeated yapping sound comes from a needy dog wanting its owner's attention.

Yelp
This short, sharp sound usually means the dog has been surprised or been hurt.

Sigh
Loud intakes of breath come from a content canine or a puppy about to fall asleep.

Grrrrr!

Perfect pitch
Low-pitched noises generally mean the dog is feeling anger or fear. High-pitched noises suggest high levels of excitement!

Woof!

Bark
A few barks are a welcome home, but lots of barking can be a warning.

Whine
A dog making a long whining sound is worrying about something it hopes the owner can fix.

Growl
Back off from a growling dog. This deep, throaty sound shows either upset or irritation.

Fast frequency
When a dog keeps repeating vocal sounds quickly, it is feeling very excited. Big breaks between sounds show a lack of interest.

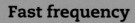

Canine characters

Dogs have different personalities. Check out these cute and crazy characters to see which one sounds most like your pet pooch.

Playful
Want to play? I've got the ball ready!

Curious
What is going on down there?

Puppy personalities

Puppies show their own personalities starting at seven weeks old. Meet the wonderful young woofers here!

Independent
This strong-minded pup likes to go its own way.

Sweet
With its gentle nature, this pup just wants lots of love!

Shy
I wish they would stop looking at me.

Forceful
You'll have to get past me first!

Loving
If I look this cute, will you cuddle with me?

Does your dog match your personality?

Eager
This enthused pup wants to please, so training is easy!

Timid
Shy guys hold back and avoid too much contact.

Social
Bring on the people and playtime!

Bossy
This determined dog likes to be the leader in charge of everything.

25

Dog's day

Dogs like to eat, play, explore, walk, and sleep! They are happiest when with their owner and don't like it when their owner goes out. Dogs take a nap and wait for their owner to return home.

Happy home
Dogs often guard their home and keep watch on what's going on throughout the day. They love to play with dog toys.

Good **morning!**

Did you know?
Dogs dream just the same way we do.

26

Afternoon **walks!**

The great outdoors

Dogs love going for walks or—even better—runs! They get to see the world as well as meeting other dogs and new people. They like it when people pay a lot of attention to them.

Evening **bedtime!**

Sleepyhead

Puppies sleep for about 15 hours a day, including naps. If you see a dog twitching while asleep, it is dreaming about the fun it had during the day.

ZZZZz

A dog's day

Morning
Wake up for a walk!

Playtime with owner

Breakfast is ready!

ZZZZz   Nap time

Afternoon
More exercise or playtime

Nap time   zZZZZ
Dinner is served!

Evening
More exercise or playtime, and one last walk!

Bedtime   zZZZZ

Dogs and humans

There is a reason why dogs are known as man's best friend. Wonderful woofers are much more than family pets. They help us to bond, love, and heal. We'd be lost without them!

Just the same

Dogs and humans have a lot in common:

 **Newborn puppies and babies** are both helpless and depend entirely on their mother for survival.

 **Dogs and people** pick up on the feelings of others and respond in the best way.

Both puppies and children enjoy playtime, and experience lots of new things very quickly.

Perfect pets

Dogs improve human health. Owners keep in shape from shared walks, while petting a dog can lower blood pressure. Dogs offer company for sad or lonely people.

93 percent of dog owners say dog walking reduces their stress levels.

Both humans and dogs

express love with affection, kindness, and lots of cuddling!

People and dogs need

plenty of sleep to be happy, as well as enjoying good food and company.

Listen up, number experts!

Dogs age faster than people. We can compare their ages by learning that the first year of a dog's life is about the same as 15 human years. The numbers slow down after the first year.

On its first birthday, a dog is like a 15-year-old human.

On its second birthday, a dog is like a 24-year-old human.

On its third birthday, a dog is like a 29-year-old human.

Every dog year after this is like 5 more years for a human.

Longest life

On average, dogs live for 13 years, but the world record was set by an Australian Cattle Dog who reached 29 years old!

Dogs with jobs

Service dogs are specially trained to help people who struggle with a disability or illness. Meet some of the dogs taking care of us in the community.

Guide dogs

These dogs work hard to help people who are blind or visually impaired. Whether in the home or on a busy street, they lead their owners around with care and safety in mind.

Hearing dogs

Trained dogs let people with hearing problems know when there is a sound, such as a doorbell. They also pick up danger signs, such as smoke alarms, then alert their owners.

Some dogs **take money out from**

Mobility-assistance dogs

If someone is in a wheelchair or has to stay in a bed, a mobility-assistance dog can help out. They do many jobs in the home, such as opening doors, helping to dress their owners, and much more.

Allergy-detection dogs

Many people have serious allergies to different foods. Allergy-detection dogs are trained to sniff out specific smells, such as peanuts, then alerting their owners to the danger.

Guide dogs are specially trained starting at two months old.

GUIDE DOG

Medical-alert dogs

People with serious illnesses may collapse suddenly when home alone. Medical-alert dogs know the signs when this is about to happen, and they make their owners seek help.

cash machines for their owners!

Hero dogs

The most brilliant and brave canines are true heroes. Dogs often work on the front line to ensure safety and save lives in real emergencies.

Did you know?
By 2017, a Labrador named Frida had rescued 53 people from natural disasters in Mexico.

Dogs can **sniff out** victims faster than the emergency services.

Hard at work

Pet power
Dogs have helped their owners in times of need by barking to raise the alarm, swimming with them to safety, or biting an attacking animal.

Rescue dogs
Search-and-rescue dogs help find people in the snow after an avalanche or in the rubble of a collapsed building.

Another day, another mountain rescue... I need a nap!

Soldiers' sidekick
Many armies and navies use trained guard dogs to protect their soldiers. These dogs can sniff out dangerous bombs and mines.

Detection dogs
Doggy detectives are trained to hunt for things. Airports and border controls rely on them to find illegal food, explosives, or drugs.

In the **doghouse**

Prepare for the arrival of your furry friend by turning your home into the **perfect pooch palace.**

Register your dog with a local vet for checkups, vaccinations, and emergencies.

Dogs depend on us for their well-being.

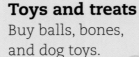

Hair care
Get a grooming kit to keep your dog's fur clean, cut, and in top condition.

Take a leash
Put a collar and leash on your dog every time you go out!

Bedtime
Choose a bed that is comfy for your pet to lie down in.

Toys and treats
Buy balls, bones, and dog toys.

New arrival

Make a list of all the equipment you need for your new pet. Be sure none of the doggie toys are so small that your dog could choke on them.

Box of delights
A dog crate provides a safe place for your pet during trips.

Bite to eat
Put food and water in two heavy dog bowls in the same place every day.

Street safety
Secure your dog with a special harness for safe travel in the car.

Lost dog
A microchip under the dog's skin contains the owner's details.

Day-to-day

House rules and routines are as important for dogs as they are for the rest of the family.

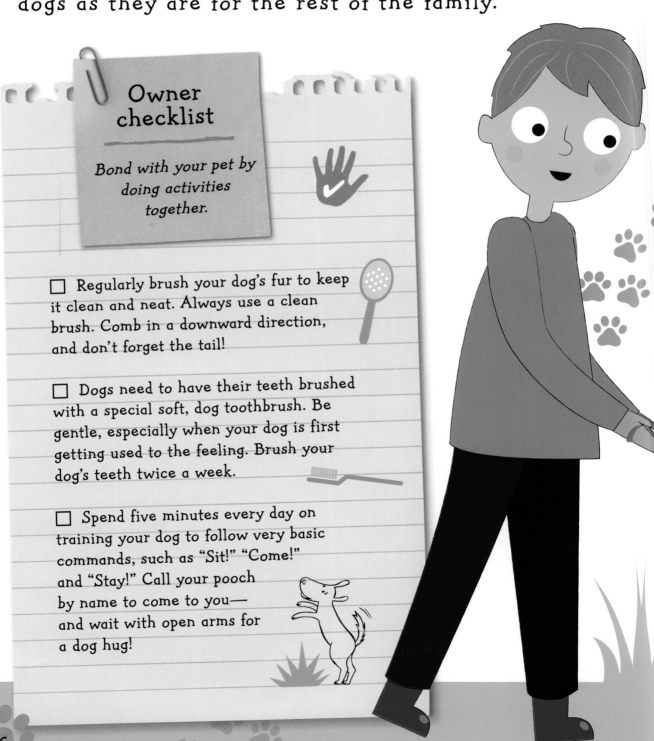

Owner checklist

Bond with your pet by doing activities together.

☐ Regularly brush your dog's fur to keep it clean and neat. Always use a clean brush. Comb in a downward direction, and don't forget the tail!

☐ Dogs need to have their teeth brushed with a special soft, dog toothbrush. Be gentle, especially when your dog is first getting used to the feeling. Brush your dog's teeth twice a week.

☐ Spend five minutes every day on training your dog to follow very basic commands, such as "Sit!" "Come!" and "Stay!" Call your pooch by name to come to you— and wait with open arms for a dog hug!

✔ Top tip

Keep your dog's **favorite treats or toys** nearby after training sessions. Pets love **reward time** and understand they are doing well as a result.

Taking charge

Sticking to rules and routines keeps day-to-day plans running smoothly. Owners who are patient and encouraging get the best results when teaching their dogs to follow rules.

Doggie checklist

These items will make your dog very well-behaved!

Wow! Looks like I've got a lot to learn...

☐ Understand and follow basic commands.

Come!

☐ Come back when called during walks!

☐ Eat and exercise when told to.

☐ Be careful in the house—don't chew or break things!

☐ Complete outdoor toilet training.

Dog's dinner

A healthy diet is important to keep your pooch in perfect condition. Pick different dog foods, but introduce new ones gradually, and always leave fresh water out. Slurp!

Growing puppies

Puppies should only eat puppy food because it's softer than adult food and doesn't need to be chewed as much, which helps smaller mouths and growing teeth. Puppy food has more protein, calcium, and fat to help tooth and bone growth.

Did you know?
80 percent of a natural dog diet is meat.

Dogs eat one or two big meals a day.

Puppies need three or four meals daily.

Doggie delights

Dogs eat dry complete food, wet complete food, or a mix of both food types.

Dry food
A good quality dry food is packed with nutrients. Dry food can be left out in a bowl all day for your dog to eat.

Top treats
Mini marrowbones are the perfect treat, packed with vitamins, minerals, and calcium to keep dogs healthy.

Wet food
This type of food has a strong smell so dogs love it. It is easy to swallow, and keeps dogs hydrated.

Sweet snack
Dry doggie biscuits can be given as a reward for good behavior every now and then.

Water
Keep a bowl of fresh, clean water out for your dog. If your dog isn't drinking enough, give it wet food.

Raisins   Grapes   Chocolate

Onions

What NOT to eat!
It may be a sweet treat for you, but chocolate is dangerous and even deadly to dogs. Other foods to avoid are onions, grapes, and raisins.

Doggie dentist
Giving your dog raw bones and marrowbone treats to crunch on helps keep their teeth and gums healthy.

Training and tricks

Start training at a young age if you want to see good behavior and even top tricks from your pet pup. With lots of encouragement, puppies learn fast. Keep those tasty dog treats ready as a welcome reward!

Quick commands

Cover the basics first. Make sure your pup understands and responds to these simple commands.

"Come!"

Your dog must know this command before it can be allowed off the leash.

Box of tricks

Now the fun starts. Once your puppy has mastered the basics, it's time to teach them tricks.

Shaking hands—or paws!

Standing up

Lying down

Puppies quickly learn the word **"Walk!"**

"Sit!"
While training, give your dog a treat each time it sits down properly.

"Stay!"
Your dog can't always come with you, so teach your dog to stay.

Older dogs are good at learning tricks since they can focus longer than pups can.

"No!"
If a dog misbehaves, be firm in telling it so.

"Walk!"
This soon becomes a dog's favorite word and they never forget it!

Practice makes perfect
Be patient with your dog, and keep practicing.

Getting ready for a walk

Fetching a ball

and will be **up and out** before long!

Terriers

Try keeping up with a terrier! These dogs have big personalities and boundless energy. Terriers need lots of exercise and enjoy being busy.

Russian Black Terrier

Airedale Terrier

Kerry Blue Terrier

Jumbo

Large

Russian Black Terrier
Bred by the Russian Army as a guard dog, this terrier is lively and brave.

Airedale Terrier
Full of courage, these terriers helped soldiers during World War I.

Kerry Blue Terrier
These loyal dogs are intelligent, brave, and make great family pets.

Irish Terrier
This dog is quick to learn and is known for its bright-red coat.

The **Russell Terrier** can jump **five times** its own **height**!

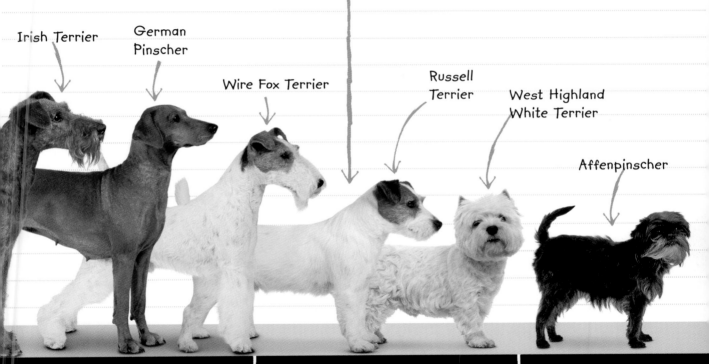

Irish Terrier

German Pinscher

Wire Fox Terrier

Russell Terrier

West Highland White Terrier

Affenpinscher

Medium

German Pinscher
Alert and fearless, these dogs make great watchdogs.

Wire Fox Terrier
These quick dogs are always ready for a game of chase!

Small

Russell Terrier
Although tiny, these dogs have lots of spirit and energy!

West Highland White Terrier
These are lively dogs.

Toy

Affenpinscher
This mini terrier enjoys the comforts of home. It's a brave guard dog, despite its size.

Airedale Terrier

Called "king of the terriers," the Airedale is one of the biggest breeds of terrier. It used to work as a river dog, hunting badgers and otters. Today the Airedale keeps busy by walking, chasing, and digging.

Long and flat head shape

Wavy topcoat covers a fluffy undercoat.

Strong, long legs support the heavy body weight.

Fact file

- **Origin:** England
- **Size:** Jumbo
- **Weight:** 40–65 lb (18–30 kg)
- **Color:** Mix of black and brown
- **Character:** Confident, intelligent, brave, and playful
- **Voice:** Big barker
- **Daily exercise:** At least one hour

West Highland White Terrier

Nicknamed "the Westie," this pure-white terrier loves life and enjoys adventure. The breed was once used to hunt rats, but is now the perfect pet.

Westies often tilt their heads to one side, as if they're asking a question!

Fur has a rough topcoat and a soft undercoat.

Powerful and strong body is packed with muscles.

Fact file

- **Origin:** Scotland
- **Size:** Small to medium
- **Weight:** 13–22 lb (6–10 kg)
- **Color:** White
- **Character:** Happy, friendly, active, and independent
- **Voice:** Very noisy
- **Daily exercise:** Up to one hour

Russell Terrier

This small breed of terrier is lively and loyal. The first Russells were working dogs taught to hunt foxes. Plenty of training and exercise are important for good behavior.

The tail is held high unless the Russell is resting.

Small, strong body

Powerful legs

Fact file

- 🌐 **Origin:** England
- 🦴 **Size:** Small
- ⚖️ **Weight:** 13–17 lb (6–8 kg)
- 🌸 **Color:** Mostly white with a mix of black or brown
- 🐾 **Character:** Energetic, brave, intelligent, and athletic
- 💬 **Voice:** Loud barks
- 🦴 **Daily exercise:** One hour of walking or running

Every Russell has an individual pattern of markings.

Its **fur** is mostly **white**.

Its **hair** is **short**, **thick**, and easy to keep **clean** with daily brushing.

Its **fur** can be **smooth** or **rough**.

Hounds

Hounds are natural leaders of the pack. Often bred to hunt, they will run after anything that catches their eye. Hang on tight when they're on a leash!

Afghan Hound

Pharaoh Hound

Greyhound

Large

Greyhound
These graceful racers can run as fast as 43 mph (70 kph).

Afghan Hound
These tall dogs have high hipbones that make them excellent at jumping.

Medium

Basset Hound
This short-legged breed makes a gentle family pet.

Pharaoh Hound
This friendly dog can be taught to smile and often blushes when excited or happy.

When following a **scent**, a **Basset Hound's** ears sweep **smells** toward its **nose** so it can smell them better.

Finnish Hound

Bruno Jura

Norwegian Elkhound

Basset Hound

Miniature Dachshund

Small

Tiny

Finnish Hound
Independent and sometimes stubborn, these hounds make great working dogs.

Bruno Jura
Perfect pets for people who like being outdoors, these dogs love to explore.

Norwegian Elkhound
Intelligent and loving, these furry dogs are full of affection for their owners.

Miniature Dachshund
Small and proud, Dachshunds are lively and loving dogs.

Norwegian Elkhound

The national dog of Norway looks like a small, cuddly wolf. This breed was once used to hunt moose and bears. Now it prefers to play in the snow.

Upright ears make this dog look alert.

Tightly curled tail sits over the back.

Thick double coat keeps it warm in cold winters.

Sturdy and strong body

Fact file

- **Origin:** Norway
- **Size:** Small
- **Weight:** 48–55 lb (21–25 kg)
- **Color:** Gray, silver

- **Character:** Strong, protective, brave, and bold
- **Voice:** Very vocal, lots of barking and howling
- **Daily exercise:** At least one hour of running

Miniature **Dachshund**

Spot the sausage! This breed is nicknamed "sausage dog" because of its long body and short legs. In the past, it was trained to sniff out rabbits in tight burrows. The Miniature Dachshund enjoys lots of company and new challenges.

Long, droopy ears

Fur can be long and wiry or short and smooth.

Long and muscular body

Stubby legs are good at digging.

Fact file

- 🜉 **Origin:** Germany
- 🡕 **Size:** Tiny
- ⚖ **Weight:** 8–11 lb (4–5 kg)
- ✻ **Color:** Any mix of brown, black, and cream

- 🐾 **Character:** Brave, independent, intelligent, and lively
- 💬 **Voice:** Loud and regular barking
- 🦴 **Daily exercise:** At least one hour of walking

Afghan Hound

Check out this silky fur coat! The Afghan Hound, from the freezing cold mountains of Afghanistan, is covered in soft fur to keep it snugly warm. This breed is relaxed and calm indoors, but athletic and active when it is time to play outside.

Slim build and flexible hips mean the hound can move fast.

Slim face

Curled tail

Long, **droopy** ears

Excellent eyesight, which helps them hunt wild animals.

Flowing fur needs regular grooming to avoid knots and tangles.

Fact file

- **Origin:** Afghanistan
- **Size:** Large
- **Weight:** 51–71 lb (24–29 kg)
- **Color:** Cream, brown, gray, or black
- **Character:** Loyal, loving, protective, and sensitive
- **Voice:** Noisy barker
- **Daily exercise:** At least one hour of walking and running

Toy dogs

Here is the proof that some good things come in small packages. Some toy dogs are breeds that don't grow very big, while others are miniature versions of larger dogs. These popular pets score high on the cute chart!

Chinese Crested Dog

Cavalier King Charles Spaniel

Pug

Large	Medium
Chinese Crested Dog These dogs are hard to impress, but when they do like someone they follow them everywhere!	**Pug** This toy breed is loyal and loving.
Cavalier King Charles Spaniel This dog is sporty and lovable, and has a tail that is always wagging.	**Shih Tzu** These dogs love being indoors and have a friendly nature.

> **Pomeranians** are also called **Pom Poms**.

Shih Tzu

Russian Toy Dog

Papillon

Pomeranian

Pekingese

Chihuahua

Small

Tiny

Pekingese
These proud dogs can be stubborn and hard to train.

Russian Toy Dog
Makes a great guard dog!

Papillon
This dog is named after the French word for "butterfly," due to the shape of its ears.

Pomeranian
Small but feisty, these dogs have loads of confidence!

Chihuahua
Tiny and loving, these dogs make great companions.

Chinese Crested Dog

Meet the Chinese Crested Dog, with silky fur only on its head, feet, and tail. This energetic dog loves climbing, jumping, and digging, before cuddling up for the night—ideally in its owner's bed!

Skin needs regular baths to stay clean.

Most of the body is bald.

Fact file

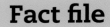

- **Origin:** Uncertain (but Chinese breeders first made this tiny version of a larger hairless dog)
- **Size:** Large
- **Weight:** Up to 12 lb (5 kg)
- **Color:** Variety of shades, from pink to black
- **Character:** Alert, friendly, loving, and sensitive
- **Voice:** May bark and howl
- **Daily exercise:** At least one hour

Cavalier King Charles Spaniel

Crowned king of the toy dogs, this breed was named after King Charles II of England and his much-loved pet spaniels. This dog wants action and affection at all times.

Big brown eyes

Long, fluffy ears

Silky, soft fur

Tail is almost always wagging.

Fact file

- **Origin:** England
- **Size:** Large
- **Weight:** 13–17 lb (6–8 kg)
- **Color:** Brown, brown and white, or black

- **Character:** Loving, playful, intelligent, and social
- **Voice:** A quiet bark
- **Daily exercise:** At least one hour

Pekingese

This small, unique dog is one of the oldest breeds. In ancient China, they were bred to look like the mythical Chinese lion. Because of this, they are nicknamed "lion dogs." Pekingese always want their own way and can misbehave as a result!

Fact file

- **Origin:** China
- **Size:** Medium
- **Weight:** 6–13 lb (3–6 kg)
- **Color:** Varieties of black, brown, gray, and cream
- **Character:** Intelligent, loving, stubborn, and proud
- **Voice:** Noisy barkers
- **Daily exercise:** At least one hour

Thick, flowing fur like a lion's mane.

In ancient China, people used to **bow** to these dogs.

Tail held high over the back.

Tiny noses can produce snoring!

Furry ears hang down.

Sporting dogs

Get-up-and-go with a sporting dog! In the past, these dogs helped find and catch birds and other creatures. Today, they will fetch just about anything they come across.

Irish Setter

Weimaraner

Wirehaired Pointing Griffon

Large

Irish Setter
This active, red-coated breed loves playing with other dogs.

Weimaraner
Strong and graceful, Weimaraners are good at tracking and retrieving.

Wirehaired Pointing Griffon
Eager to please, this hunting dog also makes an affectionate family pet.

English Setter
The oldest of the Setter breed, the English Setter is calm and reliable.

This breed is great at following the **scent** of other **animals**.

English Setter

Golden Retriever

German Spaniel

American Water Spaniel

Welsh Springer Spaniel

Cocker Spaniel

Medium	Small	Tiny
Golden Retriever Gentle and patient, this dog is now very popular as a pet. **German Spaniel** This breed was originally bred to retrieve quails.	**American Water Spaniel** Bred to retrieve ducks, this spaniel has a curly coat. **Welsh Springer Spaniel** This hard-working dog loves getting into water.	**Cocker Spaniel** The long, silky coat of this breed has made it a very popular pet.

American Water Spaniel

This unusual curly canine is the state dog of Wisconsin. Its handsome, curly coat stands out in a crowd. This high-energy explorer loves splashing in water, which is why it is also known as a water dog.

Light-brown, alert eyes

Curly, outer layer of coat keeps water out.

Webbed feet are perfect for swimming.

Fact file

- 🌐 **Origin:** USA
- ↗ **Size:** Small
- ⚖ **Weight:** 24–44 lb (11–20 kg)
- ✳ **Color:** Brown

- 🐾 **Character:** Active, affectionate, loyal, and energetic
- 💬 **Voice:** May bark if left alone
- 🦴 **Daily exercise:** At least two hours each day

Weimaraner

Think big with the Weimaraner! This dog is big in size with beautiful, blue eyes. Hunters used this breed to track deer and wolves. They gave it the nickname "Gray Ghost" after its fabulous fur and fast feet.

Light eyes can darken when excited.

Muscular and strong body

Fact file

- **Origin:** Germany
- **Size:** Large
- **Weight:** 55–84 lb (25–38 kg)
- **Color:** Silver-gray
- **Character:** Intelligent, fearless, loving, and loyal
- **Voice:** Noisy bark
- **Daily exercise:** At least an hour daily

Golden Retriever

This gorgeous breed is good as gold, making it a popular pet that loves to be part of the family. The name "retriever" comes from their past, when they brought back, or retrieved, ducks from ponds. They are still strong swimmers and enjoy jumping into water.

Soft, floppy ears

Fur can be flat or wavy.

All **retrievers** love to carry things in their **mouths**.

Powerful legs take huge strides when running.

Fact file

- ⚲ **Origin:** Scotland
- ⚲ **Size:** Medium
- ⚲ **Weight:** 55–75 lb (25–34 kg)
- ⚲ **Color:** Yellow-gold fur
- 🐾 **Character:** Friendly, social, affectionate, and happy
- 💬 **Voice:** Mostly quiet
- 🦴 **Daily exercise:** At least an hour daily

Thick, golden fur keeps out water but needs a lot of grooming.

Retrievers make great **guide dogs**.

Non sporting dogs

These unusual pooches do not fit into any of the other groups. From spots and curls to fluff and wrinkles, this mixed bag of beauties has something for everyone.

Dalmatian

Chow Chow

Chinese Shar-Pei

Large	Medium
Dalmatian	**Chinese Shar-Pei**
Dalmatian puppies are born with white fur. The black spots only start appearing at 4 weeks.	These dogs were used to guard farm animals in China, thousands of years ago.
Chow Chow	**Keeshond**
Originally used to pull sleds.	This breed is intelligent and outgoing. It mixes well with people and other pets.

Norwegian Lundehunds used to hunt **puffins**.

Keeshond

Norwegian Lundehund

Boston Terrier

Lowchen

Toy American Eskimo Dog

Toy Poodle

Small

Tiny

Norwegian Lundehund
Its front legs open wider than other dogs, allowing it to run quickly and easily.

Boston Terrier
This breed is very energetic.

Lowchen
This breed's name is German, and means "little lion."

Toy American Eskimo Dog
It is known for being an excellent guard dog.

Toy Poodle
The smallest of the Poodles, this breed is athletic, easy to train, and very intelligent.

Dalmatian

Top of the spots is the dotted Dalmatian! In the past, this athletic breed ran alongside horse-drawn carriages, guarding the passengers. They also ran ahead of fire engines to clear the way. Today, Dalmatians are better known as movie stars and family pets, but be sure you have enough energy to keep up with them!

Muscular and athletic body

Long tail is strong at the root.

Stunning short, spotted coat doesn't need a lot of care.

Long legs for fast running.

Fact file

🌐 **Origin:** Unknown

↗ **Size:** Large

⚖ **Weight:** 35–70 lb (16–32 kg)

✳ **Color:** White with black or brown spots

🐾 **Character:** Friendly, energetic, active, and loyal

💬 **Voice:** Low noise levels

🦴 **Daily exercise:** At least one hour

Poodle

The prize-winning Poodle is known for its eye-catching hairstyles! But looking this good doesn't come easy, so regular grooming is very important.

Historically, Poodles were used by hunters to fetch birds from rivers and lakes, and this breed still enjoys being in water.

Athletic and graceful body

Curly coat can be clipped into different "pom-pom" styles.

Fact file

- 🌐 **Origin:** Germany, France
- ⤢ **Size:** Mixed, depending on variety (Toy, Miniature, Standard)
- 🔔 **Weight:** Toy 4–9 lb (3–4 kg), Miniature 13–18 lb (7–8 kg), Standard 44–71 lb (20–32 kg)

- ✳️ **Color:** Varied colors but mostly black, white, cream, and gray
- 🐾 **Character:** Alert, loyal, intelligent, and affectionate
- 💬 **Voice:** Average noise levels
- 🦴 **Daily exercise:** More than one hour

Chinese Shar-Pei

Chinese Shar-Pei dogs hate feeling the cold and prefer to stay indoors. They are also upset by strangers, so family settings suit them best. In return for creature comforts, this breed gives owners lots of love and loyalty.

Short, bristly coat covers wrinkly skin folds.

Power-packed body

Mouth appears set in a permanent frown.

It has **velvety** fur.

Curved tail sits high.

Fact file

- **Origin:** China
- **Size:** Medium
- **Weight:** 40–66 lb (18–30 kg)
- **Color:** Varied colors, including black, brown, and cream
- **Character:** Affectionate, loyal, confident, and intelligent
- **Voice:** Mostly quiet
- **Daily exercise:** Up to one hour of walking

Herding dogs

Gather together for the herding dogs! This group was first used on farms to round up sheep and cattle. As family pets, these breeds still like to take charge and will try to herd their owners.

Entlebucher Mountain Dog

German Shepherd

Old English Sheepdog

Large

Entlebucher Mountain Dog
A huge Swiss breed, this dog was first bred to herd cattle.

German Shepherd
This American breed makes good guard dogs.

Old English Sheepdog
Shaggy and playful, this dog loves being with people.

Belgian Tervuren
Easy to train, highly strung Tervurens are used as police and sniffer dogs.

This breed is related to the **Dingo**.

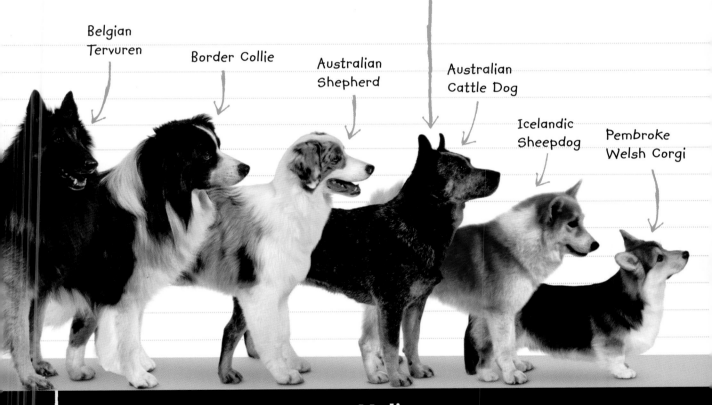

Belgian Tervuren

Border Collie

Australian Shepherd

Australian Cattle Dog

Icelandic Sheepdog

Pembroke Welsh Corgi

Medium

Border Collie
This dog is one of the best at herding sheep.

Australian Shepherd
This breed is widely used as search-and-rescue dogs.

Australian Cattle Dog
This strong dog can deal with Australia's heat.

Icelandic Sheepdog
This tough, little dog is related to huskies.

Pembroke Welsh Corgi
Corgis were bred to nip at the heels of cattle, keeping them on the move.

Pembroke Welsh Corgi

Corgis have a royal reputation! Queen Elizabeth II of the United Kingdom keeps Corgis as palace pets. In the past, this breed controlled cattle on Welsh farmland. A local legend claims that fairies used to ride into battle on Corgis!

Foxlike face

Long, upright ears

The unique back marking is called the "fairy saddle!"

Fact file

🌐 **Origin:** Wales

🦴 **Size:** Medium

⚖ **Weight:** 22–31 lb (10–14 kg)

❂ **Color:** Red, black, and brown

🐾 **Character:** Loyal, playful, friendly, and intelligent

💬 **Voice:** Big barkers

🦴 **Daily exercise:** At least one hour

Old English Sheepdog

The ultimate shaggy sheepdog needs regular haircuts to stop fur from covering its eyes. In days gone by, this big breed guided cattle to farmers' markets. Now, its sweet nature and good behavior make it a perfect family pet.

Thick and powerful body

Long, shaggy coat must be brushed carefully.

Fact file

- 🐾 **Origin:** England
- ↗ **Size:** Large
- ⚖ **Weight:** 60–100 lb (27–45 kg)
- ✿ **Color:** Gray and white
- 🐾 **Character:** Intelligent, playful, loving, and friendly
- 💬 **Voice:** Not too noisy
- 🦴 **Daily exercise:** At least one hour

Border Collie

This loyal breed works like a shepherd protecting its flock. When herding sheep in the Scottish hills, Border Collies can run more than 50 miles (80 kilometers) a day. With high energy levels, they never sit still and will round up people as well as sheep!

The **Border Collie** is thought to be the **smartest** dog breed.

Eyes are fixed in a strong stare to control the sheep.

Athletic body built for speed.

Patterned fur can be rough or smooth.

Fact file

- **Origin:** Border region between England and Scotland

- **Size:** Medium

- **Weight:** 29–44 lb (14–20 kg)

- **Color:** Black and white

- **Character:** Alert, energetic, reliable, and loyal

- **Voice:** Regular barker

- **Daily exercise:** At least two hours

Working dogs

Meet the dogs with jobs! Some breeds are trained to do different tasks to help people. They keep watch, pull heavy loads, or perform emergency rescues.

Saint Bernard

Newfoundland

Komondor

Large

Saint Bernard
This gentle giant can weigh more than a full-grown man.

Newfoundland
Bred in Canada, Newfoundlands like rescuing people in the water!

Komondor
A mighty mop on legs, the Komondor was bred to protect cattle.

Bernese Mountain Dog
Originally a livestock-guarding dog, this breed is now a popular pet.

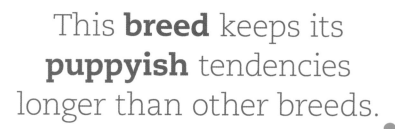

This **breed** keeps its **puppyish** tendencies longer than other breeds.

Bernese Mountain Dog

Rottweiler

Boxer

Siberian Husky

Labrador Retriever

Large

Rottweiler
Powerful and obedient, Rottweilers make great guard dogs.

Siberian Husky
The Chukchi people of Siberia used this breed for pulling sleds.

Boxer
This fun-loving family dog was first bred in Germany.

Labrador Retriever
These dogs are lovable and kind. They have lots of energy so need long walks.

Saint Bernard

If you find yourself in an emergency, call a Saint Bernard! This rescue dog was sent out in storms to sniff out and save mountain climbers buried deep in the snow. Today, the breed is a physical powerhouse with a heart of gold.

Black patches surround the eyes.

Tongue often hangs out of the mouth.

Superstrong body

Thick coat can be rough or smooth with a variety of markings.

Fact file

- **Origin:** France, Italy, and Switzerland
- **Size:** Large
- **Weight:** 132–176 lb (60–80 kg)
- **Color:** Brown and white

- **Character:** Lively, friendly, loving, and loyal
- **Voice:** Rarely barks
- **Daily exercise:** One hour

Siberian Husky

This winter wonder was first used to pull sleds for local people in snowy Siberia. With tons of strength and drive, the breed just keeps on running. It is now a popular pet breed.

Eyes are blue or brown and always alert.

Athletic body shape and powerful legs

Tough, furry feet ideal for covering hard ground.

Fact file

- **Origin:** Siberia, now in Russia
- **Size:** Large
- **Weight:** 35–60 lb (16–27 kg)
- **Color:** Varieties of black, gray, silver, and white
- **Character:** Intelligent, friendly, reliable, and playful
- **Voice:** Howler
- **Daily exercise:** At least one hour

Bernese Mountain Dog

At home in the Swiss Alps, this breed can do many jobs. Rounding up animals, dragging carts, and standing guard are all in a day's work for this heavyweight jack-of-all-trades.

White fur can form a cross shape on the tummy.

Fact file

- 🌐 **Origin:** Switzerland
- ↗ **Size:** Large
- ⚖ **Weight:** 68–115 lb (32–52 kg)
- ✳ **Color:** Black, brown, and white
- 🐾 **Character:** Loyal, affectionate, intelligent, and gentle
- 💬 **Voice:** Very little barking
- 🦴 **Daily exercise:** At least one hour

This breed almost **disappeared** in the 1800s.

A Bernese Mountain Dog makes a great pet.

Strong and sturdy body shape

Thick, long fur provides a layer of warmth in the mountains.

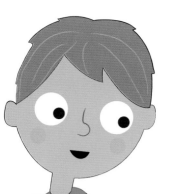

Mixed breeds
and mongrels

Some dog breeders cross two different breeds together to create a crossbreed. Dogs with more than two breeds in his or her family are called mixed breeds, mutts, or mongrels.

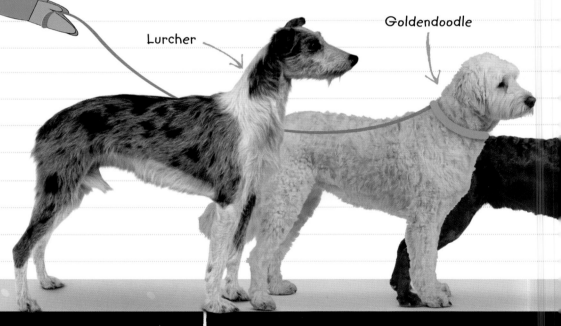

Lurcher

Goldendoodle

Jumbo

Large

Lurcher
A natural racer, lurchers are a cross between a Greyhound and a Collie or Terrier.

Goldendoodle
This Golden Retriever and Poodle cross doesn't shed fur.

Labradinger
This is a cross between a Labrador and an English Springer Spaniel.

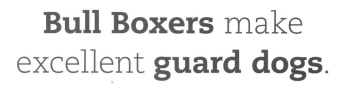

Bull Boxers make excellent **guard dogs**.

Labradinger

Bull Boxer

Labradoodle

Cockerpoo

Bichon Yorkie

Chiweenie

Medium	Small	Toy
Bull Boxer This cross has Staffordshire Bull Terrier and Boxer blood. **Labradoodle** A Labrador and a Poodle make up this popular cross.	**Cockerpoo** A Cocker Spaniel and Poodle cross, Cockerpoos make very endearing pets.	**Chiweenie** A playful Chihuahua and Dachshund mix. **Bichon Yorkie** A Bichon Frise and Yorkshire Terrier cross.

Labradoodle

What do you get if you cross a Labrador with a Poodle? A lovely Labradoodle! This mixed breed was designed to have a nonshedding coat to help people suffering from dog allergies. A Labradoodle has the energy of a Labrador and the intelligence of a Poodle.

Strong, athletic body

Fact file

- **Origin:** Australia
- **Size:** Standard, Medium, and Miniature
- **Weight:** 22–88 lb (10–40 kg)
- **Color:** Variety of colors
- **Character:** Intelligent, loyal, social, and affectionate
- **Voice:** May bark or howl
- **Daily exercise:** At least one hour

Fur does not shed much compared to other dogs.

Ears that droop downward

Coat can be wavy or curly.

This **dog's** coat **needs** two weekly **brushings**.

Chiweenie

Canines don't come cuter than the Chiweenie. This adorable mix of the Chihuahua and the Dachshund is nicknamed the "Mexican Hotdog!" The Chiweenie scores high for energy and enthusiasm.

Big ears compared to the head size

Long body of the Daschund

Coat is easy to take care of.

Fact file

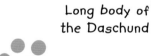

- 🌐 **Origin:** North America
- ↗ **Size:** Small
- ⚖ **Weight:** 8–12 lb (4–5 kg)
- ❋ **Color:** Can vary

- 🐾 **Character:** Friendly, playful, affectionate, and energetic
- 💬 **Voice:** Vocal
- 🦴 **Daily exercise:** At least one hour

Mongrels

Many pooches are produced by different breeds coming together, without people helping their development. These natural, mixed-breed dogs are called mutts, or mongrels—anything goes in this group!

Quiz—picking the perfect pooch

Imagine **choosing a dog** because it **looks like you** or has the **same personality**! Experts think we **do exactly that.** Take this **quiz** to see if your **perfect pooch** is a canine version of you!

1. What is your favorite type of dog?
- ☐ **a)** Long-legged racer
- ☐ **b)** Hairy heavyweight
- ☐ **c)** Miniature, but mighty

2. What personality traits do you look for in a dog?
- ☐ **a)** Up and at 'em! Think playful and active
- ☐ **b)** By your side! Think reliable and loyal
- ☐ **c)** Don't forget me! Think alert and attention seeking

3. How much noise do you want to hear?
- ☐ **a)** Quiet please!
- ☐ **b)** Only when necessary
- ☐ **c)** Bring on the barking!

4. How often do you like to go for walks?
- ☐ **a)** Walk? I run!
- ☐ **b)** One big walk a day
- ☐ **c)** A short walk is more than enough

5. Do you consider yourself high energy?
- ☐ **a)** "Always on-the-go" describes me
- ☐ **b)** A nice balance of playtime and downtime
- ☐ **c)** Staying indoors is perfect for me

I think I know now!

6. Do you like cuddling on the couch?
- ☐ **a)** There's no time to sit still
- ☐ **b)** Is there room for a big one?
- ☐ **c)** Snuggled on the sofa… permanently

If you answered mostly a's, go for:
A *sporting dog.* These breeds want endless action and activity, so just be sure you can keep up!

If you answered mostly b's, go for:
A *working dog.* Depend on these big breeds to protect you, but don't forget they need a lot of care and walks!

If you answered mostly c's, go for:
A *toy dog.* These breeds are small and sweet, but they are also noisier than the average dog and demand a lot of your time!

Glossary

Allergy A bad reaction to fur or another substance, which usually brings on watery eyes and sneezing.

Breed A type of dog with specific characteristics.

Breeder A person who raises and develops a type of animal.

Canine A dog or something that is doglike.

Carnivore An animal with biting teeth that eats a diet of meat.

Command To give an order or instruction to be followed.

Companion A friend or someone you spend a lot of time with.

Crossbreed A dog whose parents are of two different breeds.

Disability A medical condition that affects a person's life.

Domestic An animal that is taken care of by people.

Emergency A sudden and serious situation in which action is required.

Fleas Tiny insects that jump from creature to creature to feed on their blood.

Flexible Something that bends very well without breaking.

Groom To brush and clean fur.

Guard To keep watch to ensure protection or stop an escape.

Herd To gather a group of animals together.

Hunt To chase after another animal to catch it.

Instinct An animal's typical response in different situations.

Litter A group of baby puppies born to the same mother.

Microchip A small device on which information is stored.

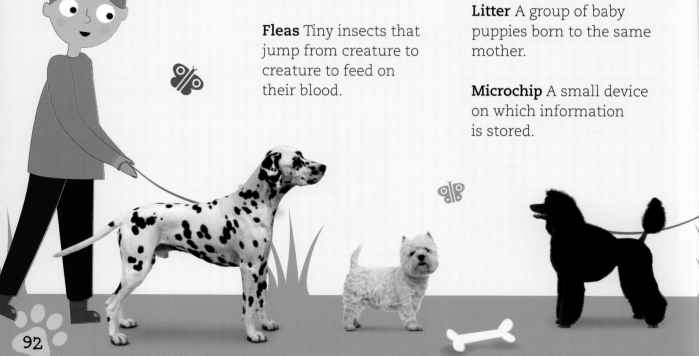

Mixed breed A dog whose background is a variety of breeds.

Mongrel A dog produced from a natural mix of different breeds.

Mutt A dog produced from a natural mix of different breeds.

Native Born or coming from a specific place.

Nutrients Different substances needed to maintain health, growth, and development.

Prey An animal that is hunted and killed by another animal for food.

Protein A substance needed for a healthy diet, found in food such as meat and eggs.

Routine A regular order of activities following the same time frame.

Socialization Mixing animals or people together so they learn how to behave in group situations.

Species A type of animal.

Stray A once-domesticated animal that has left its home and lives without an owner.

Tame An animal that is used to having contact with people.

Therapy A form of treatment designed to help and improve the well-being of people.

Weaning The process by which very young puppies move on from their mother's milk to meat.

Wild An animal living free without any help from people.

Index

Acknowledgments

DK would like to thank:

Shalini Agrawal and Shambhavi Thatte for editorial work; Lizzie Davey for additional editorial; Nidhi Mehra and Shipra Jain for design work; Eleanor Bates, Elaine Hewson, and Kitty Glavin for additional design; Dheeraj Singh for CTS; Rajesh Singh and Vijay Kandwa for hi-res image work; Rituraj Singh and Surya Sarangi for picture research; and Helen Peters for preparing the index.

The publisher would like to thank the following for their kind permission to reproduce their photographs:

Key: a=above; b=below/bottom; c=centre; f=far; l=left, r=right, t=top.

1 iStockphoto.com: cynoclub (b). **4 Dorling Kindersley:** Jerry Young (ca, crb). **Dreamstime.com:** Roughcollie (clb). **5 123RF.com:** Iakov Filimonov (c). **Dorling Kindersley:** Jerry Young (cl, crb). **Dreamstime.com:** Dreamzdesigner (clb/map). **6-7 123RF.com:** (c). **7 Dreamstime.com:** Roughcollie (tc, ca, c). **8 iStockphoto.com:** 3drenderings (clb). **10 iStockphoto.com:** cynoclub (b); VioletaStoimenova (cra). **11 Dreamstime.com:** Supertrooper / alex (cla/Grass Background). **iStockphoto.com:** amaturner (cra); Vivienstock (cla); tap10 (br). **12 Dreamstime.com:** Supertrooper / alex (clb/Grass Background). **16 123RF.com:** robodread (cra). **17 iStockphoto.com:** igorr1 (c). **18 iStockphoto.com:** damedeeso (b). **19 Dreamstime.com:** Isselee (cl/Shetland Sheepdog). **20 Dreamstime.com:** Alhovik (ca). **21 iStockphoto.com:** MirasWonderland (cla). **22 iStockphoto.com:** cynoclub (bc); nicolas_ (l). **23 iStockphoto.com:** dageldog (r). **24 123RF.com:** mdorottya (bc). **iStockphoto.com:** mphillips007 (cl); NeilLockhart (cra). **25 iStockphoto.com:** GlobalP (cl); Lightstar59 (cr). **26 123RF.com:** bonzami emmanuelle (tr). **27 iStockphoto.com:** dageldog (tc). **28-29 iStockphoto.com:** skynesher (b). **30 Dreamstime.com:** Supertrooper / alex (cla/Grass Background); Jeroen Van Den Broek / Vandenbroek29 (cla). **31 Dreamstime.com:** Supertrooper / alex (tl/Grass Background); Jeroen Van Den Broek (tl). **iStockphoto.com:** FatCamera (crb); fokusgood (tr). **32 iStockphoto.com:** Philartphace (bl); suc (ca); seraficus (crb).

33 123RF.com: Monika Wisniewska (bl). **iStockphoto.com:** casiano (crb); Figure8Photos (t). **35 123RF.com:** Elnur Amikishiyev (cr). **36 Dreamstime.com:** Evellade / (Dalevina) (Art A Lot) (bc); Stocksolutions (cl). **37 Dreamstime.com:** Evellade / (Dalevina) (Art A Lot) (br/Dog illustration); Stocksolutions (crb). **40-41 iStockphoto.com:** nycshooter (b). **42 Dorling Kindersley:** Tracy Morgan (cl). **43 iStockphoto.com:** Illustrious (br). **45 iStockphoto.com:** Illustrious (br). **47 iStockphoto.com:** Illustrious (br). **49 iStockphoto.com:** Illustrious (br). **51 iStockphoto.com:** Illustrious (br). **53 iStockphoto.com:** Illustrious (br). **55 iStockphoto.com:** Illustrious (br). **57 iStockphoto.com:** Illustrious (br). **58-59 iStockphoto.com:** fotojagodka (c). **61 iStockphoto.com:** Illustrious (br). **63 iStockphoto.com:** Illustrious (br). **65 iStockphoto.com:** Illustrious (br). **67 iStockphoto.com:** Illustrious (br). **69 iStockphoto.com:** Illustrious (br). **73 iStockphoto.com:** Illustrious (br). **75 iStockphoto.com:** Illustrious (br). **77 iStockphoto.com:** Illustrious (br). **81 iStockphoto.com:** Illustrious (br). **83 iStockphoto.com:** Illustrious (br). **85 123RF.com:** Erik Lam / eriklam (clb/Labradoodle). **Dreamstime.com:** William Wise (crb/Chiweenie). **iStockphoto.com:** Illustrious (br). **86-87 123RF.com:** Erik Lam / eriklam (c). **87 iStockphoto.com:** Illustrious (br). **88 Dreamstime.com:** William Wise (c). **89 iStockphoto.com:** Illustrious (br). **90 123RF.com:** mdorottya (cl). **91 Alamy Stock Photo:** Yuri Arcurs / InsadCo Photography (cl). **94 iStockphoto.com:** cynoclub (bc). **96 iStockphoto.com:** MirasWonderland (b)

Cover images: *Front:* **Ardea:** Jean-Michel Labat crb; **Fotolia:** Paul Cotney br, Eric Isselee cra; Warren Photographic Limited: bl; *Back:* **Fotolia:** Eric Isselee tc, Viorel Sima tr; **iStockphoto.com:** nycshooter tl; **Warren Photographic Limited:** br

All other images © Dorling Kindersley.
For further information see: www.dkimages.com